SHOW UP FOR YOU

SHOW UP FOR YOU
THE STAGE IS WAITING FOR YOU

Dr. Judy Mandrell

PURPOSEPALS PUBLISHING

SHOW UP FOR YOU
Copyright 2024, Judy Mandrell
Printed in the United States of America.
ISBN: 979-8-218-56769-9
Library of Congress Control Number: 2024926155
Editor: Danette McBride and Dr. Brenda Jarmon
Cover Designer: Brittany Rockwell
Production Manager: Kimi Johnson

All rights reserved. No part of this book may be used or reproduced in any manner whatsoever without the written permission of the publisher, and or author except in the case of brief quotations embodied in critical articles and reviews.

Although every precaution has been taken in preparation of this book, the publisher and author assume no responsibility for errors or omissions. Nor is any liability assumed for damages resulting from the use of the information contained herein.

PurposePals Publishing books may be ordered through booksellers or by contacting PurposePals.
hello@purposepalsllc.com
purposepalsllc.com

TO MY DAUGHTER
DR. JUDTH RENEE MANDRELL

Judith Renee is a name I chose for her, but perhaps she should have been named Esther, a strong, tenacious Jewish woman who stood up for her people and averted genocide. This is my Judy, a fighter for justice within the church and community. She believes in righteousness and is driven by dreams and visions. Judy is a lover of all people, always ready to help and teach others that they can achieve their goals. With God on your side, nothing is impossible. My Judy loves the Lord, and it's evident in her daily life. She shows compassion for others, accepting them where they are while encouraging them to strive for more. My Judy is a leader of leaders.

Our motto: Help someone along the way, and your life will not be in vain.

Love always,
Momma, Dr. Irma Hunter Wesley

Praise for
SHOW UP FOR YOU

"Show Up for You" by Dr. Judy Mandrell is a masterful launch pad of life that deliberately ignites your passion and purpose to lead with confidence and authenticity. Her narrative offers a warmth and wealth of wisdom plus relevant examples that motivate personal success. The chapters captivate your attention while propelling you to visualize your greatness, take action, and intentionally find ways to celebrate your self-worth. This book speaks to every level of leadership and provides practical tools to apply in your life daily. The steps and strategies the author gives to help initially develop or simply enhance a working plan to succeed at showing up, is life-changing. This is a must-read for anyone interested in excelling as a leader.

With Love and Excitement,
-Danette McBride "Covenant Friend"
Deputy Director of Infrastructure Services
Department of Financial Services
Tallahassee, FL

When selecting a book that truly brings out your best, it's essential to choose one that addresses the full spectrum of your personal needs.

"Show Up for You" is designed to do just that. It not only guides, motivates, and inspires, but also empowers you to take charge of your own journey. Whether you require a gentle nudge or a bold wake-up call, this book provides the support you need. It's a cutting-edge motivational tool, crafted to elevate you to the next level of personal growth and success. When you have the opportunity to show up, you'll now have the tool to guide you in the right direction. Now is the time to Show Up for You! Brava Dr Judy!

Kind regards,
-Baroness Cynthia Holden-Sister
Managing Director of
Blacque Baroness Productions
Edinburgh, United Kingdom

My sister Judy—the evangelist, prayer warrior, supporter, and motivator—is a force to be reckoned with. If Judy is in your corner, you'll never fail. She leads by example and is a woman of tenacity, strength, dreams, and love. If it's possible, Judy will make it happen. We've been close since birth, and I'm incredibly proud of her. Her book, Show Up for You, teaches you step-by-step that no matter what, you can do it. This is just the beginning of many more books to come from my sister, Dr. Judy R. Mandrell. Remember, you can do it!

Love,
-Tonya Wesley Pile, your baby sister

I wanted to take a moment to celebrate your incredible accomplishments - the publication of your book "Show Up For YOU." Your words have the power to inspire and uplift readers who are looking for guidance. Your unique perspective, vulnerability and insight will resonate with those who read it. I can't wait to see the impact it will create. Keep writing, keep believing and keep celebrating the beauty of self-love. Your passion is contagious!

Love,
-Dr. Tracy Sheffield

Dr. Judy Mandrell has a deep love for God, her family, her church and her community. As someone who knows her personally, she is not only an author but a powerful speaker who has inspired audiences with her words and inspiration. Judy brings that same energy to her book, "Show Up for You," a guide that is both practical and spiritual and a testament to Judy's love for God, her leadership and her commitment to sharing that love with her readers.

-Anna Johnson Riedel, Television Consultant

"Show Up for You" by Dr. Judy Mandrell is an amazing book for any leader wanting to look introspectively at everything they know and have learned about leading others. Great leaders must look deep within themselves and as the book conveys "show up" for themselves to be a leader of people. Dr. Mandrell compels the exploration of leadership and the core principles of authentic leadership. The book allows one to begin the journey of being that transformative leader one always hoped to be.

-Asst. Sheriff Ron Cave
Undersheriff
Leon County Sheriff's Department
Tallahassee, FL 32304
www.leoncountyso.com

"Show Up for You" is an inspiring guide for leaders who often prioritize the needs of others while neglecting their own well-being. With practical advice, Dr. Mandrell encourages leaders to reclaim their own space and time, emphasizing that true leadership begins with self-care and self-awareness. This book serves as a strong reminder that showing up for oneself is not just a necessity but a critical foundation for effectively showing up for others while leading with integrity, balance, and authenticity. It's a call for leaders who show up to self up!

-Mr. Wayne Salter
Commissioner of the
Department of Health and Human Services
North Dakota

In her debut book, "Show up for you: The Stage is Waiting for you," Dr. Judy Mandrell masterfully weaved leadership coaching, real life applications, and the metaphor of a superhero against the backdrop of tearing down societal obstacles and perceived personal flaws. With vivid descriptions and a keen eye for detail, Dr. Mandrell puts the power of authenticity into action. This book offers steps to unleash suppressed potentials and share the diversity of gifts not only within your inner circle, but also to the world. The book's theme of success is threaded throughout, especially in the areas that are commonly seen as weak spots: vulnerability, self-imperfections, and the power of your voice. Each section of the book is gripping and emotionally charged, keeping readers engaged from the first page to the last.

At the end of each chapter there is a section for reflections that will help with self-discovery on the journey of discovering your true self. This book is compelling and a fresh voice that stands out in a time when authentic leadership is needed in a world that is volatile, uncertain, complex, and ambiguous. "Show Up For You" is a promising start for Dr. Mandrell, marking her as a new author to watch in the literary world.

-Chief of Staff - Dr. Argatha Gilmore
Leon County Sheriff Department
Supervisor Of Women
Western Florida Jurisdiction
Church of God in Christ

"Show Up For You" is a must have - must read for all of us who pour so much into others. Each chapter invites the reader to look deep within themselves and reflect with direction and purpose. I found myself going back to my reflections and growing through every thought. Don't miss this important opportunity to show up for yourself!!

Most Sincerely,
-Dr. Michelle Gayle, Leon County Superintendent of Schools/Deputy Superintendent

"Show Up for You" by Dr. Judy Mandrell is an uplifting and practical guide that encourages readers to embrace and enhance their authentic selves and lead with confidence. Mandrell emphasizes the importance of self-awareness, the power of presence, the acceptance of imperfections, and the courage to use one's voice in all areas of life. Mandrell's compassionate and empowering approach invites readers to step into their full potential, making this book a worthwhile read for those seeking growth, confidence, and a deeper connection with their true selves. Through a blend of personal insights, actionable advice, and reflection exercises, the book provides a comprehensive guide for personal growth and leadership development. It is an invaluable resource for anyone seeking to strengthen their self-leadership and live a more intentional and fulfilling life.

Sincerely submitted,
-Dr. Susanna Miller, Ed. D.

"Show Up For You" is a deliciously presented recipe for deepening your understanding of who you truly are and the unique gifts only you can give, leading you on a delightful and insightful journey toward self-discovery so that you can offer those uniquely precious gifts, even more generously, to others.

-Drs. Michelle Mitcham & Kerry McCord

Dr. Judy Mandrell's Book, "Show Up for YOU", is 5-STAR! It is a book that is so great that it will completely bring you into its pages and illuminate wisdom at whatever stage of life you find yourself. One feels the love and caring pouring out from Dr. Mandrell's heart on each page. Dr. Mandrell reminds us that true leadership begins at the heart, with self-love and authenticity. The book contains thought-provoking exercises and action steps designed for the reader to truly connect with themselves on many levels. If you've been searching on HOW to improve your sense of self-worth, this book provides step-by-step direction. The exercises will help tap into your true, authentic self and inner power. This is the book that was divinely inspired to cultivate leaders who realize their God-given gifts. A must-read for those who want to show up more fully in their own lives!

-Mayor Pro Tem Commissioner Curtis Richardson

Dr. Judy Mandrell's 'Show Up for You' is a powerful, soul-stirring call to rise-up and take your rightful place! This isn't just another self-help book; it's a divine mandate designed to shake the very foundations of your life and propel you into your purpose. Dr. Mandrell takes you by the hand and walks you through the valleys of doubt, fear, and self-neglect, only to bring you to a place of empowerment, healing, and purpose. She reminds us that before we can lead others, we must first lead ourselves—boldly, authentically, and unapologetically.

Her words will stir the greatness that God has placed within you and challenge you to show up, stand up, and speak up for the destiny that's been waiting on you. It's a must-read for anyone who desires to improve their leadership skills and live empowered to get to their Next!

Dr. Towanda Davila-Davis, ThD, MRM, MTh, CPM
Pastor Elevate Tallahassee

SHOW UP FOR YOU is a transformative and empowering guide that encourages readers to prioritize their authentic selves and personal growth in their everyday lives. The author masterfully blends practical advice and actionable steps to help readers reconnect with their true selves, recognize their unique value, and harness the power of their authentic voice. With a compassionate and motivating tone, the book underscores the importance of **showing up for oneself**, not just for personal well-being but also for nurturing healthier relationships in all areas of life. Ideal for anyone feeling overwhelmed or disconnected, SHOW UP FOR YOU is a must-read groundbreaking guide for those ready to take control of their lives and embrace the ongoing journey of growth, learning, and self-discovery.

Dr. Brenda "BJ" Jarmon, PhD

TABLE OF CONTENTS

ACKNOWLEDGEMENTS xiv
PREFACE xvi
FOREWORD xviii
INTRODUCTION xxiii

CHAPTER ONE: SHOW UP FOR YOU

SHOW UP FOR YOU 24
CHAPTER ONE REFLECTIONS
DEFINING YOUR HERO 28
OVERCOMING CHALLENGES 29
BUILDING CONFIDENCE 30
SETTING GOALS 31
SELF-CARE 32
AFFIRMATIONS 33
ACTION PLAN 34
PERSONAL NOTES 38

CHAPTER TWO: CREATED TO BE YOU

CREATED TO BE YOU 42
CHAPTER TWO REFLECTIONS
SELF-REFLECTION 45
PURPOSE EXPLORATION 45
CANVAS OF AUTHENTICITY 46
DANCING ACROSS LIFE'S STAGE 50
ACTION STEPS 52
PERSONAL NOTES 54

CHAPTER THREE: YOU ARE NEEDED

YOU ARE NEEDED 58
CHAPTER THREE REFLECTIONS
YOUR UNIQUE QUALITIES 63
VALUES 64
YOUR DESIRED IMPACT 65
YOUR IDEAL OPPORTUNITIES 66

YOUR PERSONAL BRAND 67
ACTION PLAN... 68
IDENTIFYING YOUR VALUE PROPOSITION 69
UNDERSTANDING YOUR TARGET AUDIENCE......................... 70
MATCHING YOUR OFFERINGS.. 71
CREATING A COMPELLING OFFER.. 72
DELIVERING EXECPTIONAL VALUE 73
DISCOVERING YOUR UNIQUE ABILITIES................................. 74
IDENTIFYING YOUR TARGET AUDIENCE 75
CREATING YOUR PLATFORM 76
BUILDING YOUR AUDIENCE 77
MEASURING YOUR IMPACT 78
PERSONAL NOTES 80

CHAPTER FOUR: THE STRENGTH OF IMPERFECTIONS

THE STRENGTH OF IMPERFECTION 84
CHAPTER THREE REFLECTIONS
SELF-REFLECTION 88
DISCOVERING YOUR IDENTITY 89
BUILDING SELF-CONFIDENCE 90
EMBRACING YOUR TRUE SELF 91
REFLECTIONS 92
PERSONAL NOTES 94

CHAPTER FIVE: YOUR VOICE MUST BE HEARD

YOUR VOICE MUST BE HEARD 98
CHAPTER FIVE REFLECTIONS
UNDERSTANDING YOUR VOICE 103
FINDING YOUR AUDIENCE 104
CRAFTING YOUR MESSAGE 105
DELIVERING YOUR MESSAGE... 106
MEASURING IMPACT 108

LEARNING AND GROWTH	109
DISCOVERING YOUR VOICE	110
FINDING YOUR VOICE	111
FINDING YOUR AUDIENCE	112
MAKING YOUR VOICE HEARD	113
LISTENING AND LEARNING	114
REFLECTIONS	115
PERSONAL NOTES	116

CONCLUSION: YOUR JOURNEY BEGINS NOW

MEET THE AUTHOR	125
GET IN TOUCH	127

ACKNOWLEDGEMENTS

THANK YOU FOR HELPING ME…YES YOU!

Thank you, God, for creating me in Your image and likeness. Your choice to make me Your servant is a gift beyond measure. Empowered by Christ, I love and serve others. His faith in me is humbling and inspiring. My life belongs to Him, and I owe Him everything.

Mom, you've been my guiding light. Your love, service, and confidence have shaped who I am. Thank you for teaching me the importance of giving back and helping others. I'm grateful for your belief in me and my ability to make a difference. I vow to honor your legacy and make you proud. I love you.

Gerald, you're the best husband a woman could ask for. Your love and support have made all the difference. Thank you for believing in me and helping me achieve my dreams. I'm so excited to share this book with you and the world. I love you.

Brittany Renee Mandrell, R.I.P., everyday I think about you and strive to train future leaders in your honor. This book is for you, sweetheart.

To my siblings, Sylvester, Veronica, Robin, Nate, Cindy, Angus, Tonya, Dennis, Carolyn (daughter/sister/best friend), Doug, Michelle, Covenant friend-Danette, Marcella, Priscilla, Towanda, my nieces, nephews, godchildren, cousins, aunts, uncles, spiritual father, Bishop John Young, Sr, spiritual mom, Mother D.K. Richardson, Faye, Lori, and all my family – THANK YOU! Tonya, my soul twin, THANK YOU!

To all those who have been there for me, supported me, believed in me, cheered me on, opened doors for me, prayed for me, traveled with me, listened to me talk about this book for years, thank you.

To those who read the earlier version, gave feedback, and submitted early reviews, THANK YOU!

To my sister Baroness Cynthia Holden, your twelve-hour sacrifice during

Thanksgiving eight years ago started me seeing this book unfold. Thank you for never giving up on me or my vision. THANK YOU.

To the greatest publisher ever, Kimi Johnson of PurposePals Publishing, THANK YOU for seeing this book in the hands of thousands of people worldwide. I recommend Kimi to everyone who dreams of writing a book.

To Priscilla Jean-Louis, THANK YOU for creating the beautiful image that has drawn people into the soul of this book. Your creativity and passion are evident in every poster, flyer, ad, video, and picture.

To Danette, thank you so much for always listening, reading, adjusting, critiquing, envisioning and help me to give birth to this dream of releasing my book.

To my goddaughter, Kameryn Davis, thank you for capturing the vision of "SHOW UP FOR YOU" on a napkin as I talked. Your ability to draw from your heart is truly special. The image you created perfectly embodies the essence of this book. Kameryn, the book is here! THANK YOU.

To everyone who will purchase this book, thank you. I see you soaring in the future!

THANK YOU EVERYONE!!!!

PREFACE

Leadership is often viewed through the lens of titles and roles—CEOs, managers, pastors, directors, and politicians. But leadership is much more than a position; it's a way of being, a way of showing up in the world. Whether you're leading a team at work, guiding your family, mentoring a friend, or simply striving to lead yourself through life's challenges, you are a leader.

This book was born out of the realization that many of us, regardless of our formal roles, struggle with showing up fully and authentically for ourselves. We often put others first, sacrificing our own well-being, and in doing so, we diminish our ability to lead effectively. Whether in corporate boardrooms, nonprofit organizations, religious institutions, community groups, or within the walls of our own homes, the struggle is the same: How do we show up as our true selves, for ourselves, and how do we lead from a place of authenticity?

This book is a call to action for everyone who has ever doubted their worth, questioned their abilities, or felt the need to conform to external expectations. It's a reminder that true leadership begins with self-awareness and authenticity. By embracing who you truly are, you not only enhance your ability to lead others but also unlock your full potential as a leader in any sphere of life.

As you journey through these pages, you'll find not just stories and reflections, but also practical exercises and actionable steps designed to help you transition from knowledge to application. Whether you're a corporate executive, a community organizer, a parent, or someone simply trying to lead a more intentional life, this book is meant to be a guide—a companion on your journey to becoming the leader you were always meant to be.

It's time to step into your power, own your stage, and lead with the confidence that only comes from being unapologetically you. Leadership is not just for the few— it's for everyone. And that includes you.

FOREWORD

I have known Judy Mandrell for over 45 years. We have been blessed to have been happily married for 43 of those years. As a healthcare professional and minister, I have learned to appreciate more the psychological development of individuals watching her as she ministers to others.

I have personally experienced her love and care for the welfare and personal development of countless individuals. She does not consider personal development as a destination, but an ongoing intentional process. She studies constantly to improve herself so that she will be equipped to empower others.

The importance of you is valuable to her. Therefore, her emphasis in life is to improve every person's worth and to increase each person's awareness of their importance. I have experienced this with her as she engages every waiter or waitress that we encounter at a restaurant. No one is small or insignificant in her life. We all have value and worth!

It is the genuine love and care that she has in her heart that drives her to inspire others to greatness. She does not meet a stranger; she has a welcoming spirit that personally entreats people and appreciates their worth. The only thing that she sees in an individual's life is greatness and the potential for excellence. She sees more in you than you realize, therefore, her goal becomes her focus to cause you to fulfill your inward potential and make the impact that God has determined for you to make in life.

To sum up Judy Mandrell is expressed in the character of who she really is, a true natural born leader. Her leadership is super exceptional. And, although she has a natural propensity of great leadership skills, she studies and equips her natural abilities by sitting as a student of well-known leadership gurus, such as John Maxwell, Simon Sinek, Les Brown, and Samuel Chand. The previous qualities that I have mentioned prove that she is one of the best leaders that anyone could follow, simply because she leads with passion, love, and a great commitment to excellence.

Great leadership is born from a heart of great followship. Until you learn how to commit to another's vision, your personal vision becomes extremely difficult to achieve. Jesus states in Luke 16:12, "And if ye have not been faithful in that which is another man's, who shall give you that which is your own?" Her submission to others has paved the way to her greatness and I am proud to observe and even follow her in her endeavors, submitting to her leadership. This is why I have her serving along with me in ministry.

Show Up For You is a hallmark of her life and her intentional emphasis in building the confidence and self-esteem of both the men and women that she encounters. Meeting her is the best thing that can happen to any person's life, for she has a warm and welcoming spirit that invites you into excellence. Therefore, I invite you to prepare for an experience of your life as you read, study, and digest the principles that she provides for you in this book. Prepare yourself for more to come, for this book will leave you hungry for greater growth.

If you do not care about yourself, this book will not matter. But, if you want to improve upon yourself, this is the best book for you. Everyone that she has become engaged with should honestly report how much better their life has been because of her involvement in their life. So, get ready for growth, for this book is designed to highlight you for the better!

Dr. Gerald Mandrell
Your Loving Husband

*This book is dedicated to Mother, Dr. Irma Hunter Wesley, my beloved mother, whose unwavering love and support have shaped who I am.
Mr. Sylvester G. Wesley, my father, whose memory continues to inspire me.
Brittany Renee' Mandrell, my daughter, whose light shines brightly in my heart.
And to everyone who is ready to embrace their authenticity, potential, and make an impeccable difference without hesitation to: SHOW UP FOR YOU!*

The world needs you to show up.

INTRODUCTION

Leadership is often seen as the ability to inspire and influence others, but at its core, leadership is about showing up. It's about being present, authentic, and true to yourself in every situation. For many, this can be a daunting task. The pressures of leading an organization, a family, a community, or even oneself can lead to self-doubt and a tendency to conform to what others expect rather than embracing who we truly are.

This book is written for everyone who struggles with showing up for themselves. It's for those who find it easier to support others than to celebrate their own achievements, who feel the weight of expectations and sometimes lose sight of their own worth. Whether you're in a formal leadership role, guiding a family, mentoring others, or simply trying to lead your own life with intention, the challenges of leadership are universal, and so are the solutions.

In the chapters that follow, you'll be invited to explore the unique qualities that make you the leader you are—regardless of your role or title. You'll be challenged to embrace your imperfections, to use your voice boldly, and to step into your role with authenticity and confidence. This book is not just about self-awareness; it's about action. It's about moving from understanding who you are to applying that knowledge in ways that transform your life and the lives of those around you.

You'll find reflection prompts, exercises, and practical advice designed to help you integrate the lessons from each chapter into your daily life. The goal is to empower you to lead with your whole self, to show up fully for yourself so that you can show up fully for others.

As you begin this journey, remember leadership is not about perfection; it's about presence. It's about being the best version of yourself and leading others to do the same. Whether you're leading a company, a community, a family, or just yourself, your voice, your story, your presence—they all matter. And the world needs you to show up.

Chapter 1
Show Up for You

In the grand tapestry of life, many people have a natural inclination to cheer and support others through life's triumphs and tribulations while inadvertently neglecting themselves. Whether leading a team at work, guiding your family, mentoring friends, or simply striving to navigate your own path, this tendency can limit your ability to lead effectively. Consistently showing up for others without giving yourself the same level of care and support can diminish your effectiveness, no matter the context.

Now is the time to make an active choice, right here, right now, to be your own superhero. Thriving and leading with authenticity begins with recognizing that you are as deserving of your own support as those you guide. In the intricate threads of our existence, many of us find fulfillment in being the supporter, the cheerleader for others' journeys. As a parent, partner, friend, or leader in any capacity, giving endlessly to others while neglecting your own needs often becomes second nature. However, this imbalance can lead to burnout and a loss of personal fulfillment.

Challenging this imbalance requires a paradigm shift—a call to action to become your own superhero. Imagine donning the cape and taking center stage in your own life. This shift from passive observance to active participation in your journey is essential. Whether you're leading others or simply yourself, showing up for you directly impacts your ability to show up for others.

RECOGNIZING THE POWER OF THE PRESENT MOMENT IS CRUCIAL

It's time to break free from the constraints of societal and personal expectations and actively choose self-celebration as a means of empowerment. By prioritizing your well-being, you not only enhance your ability to lead but also set a powerful example for those around you—whether they are colleagues, family members, or friends. Often, we compare ourselves to others, feeling 'less than' in various aspects of our lives—not smart enough, thin enough, or financially savvy enough. The voice inside your head that stops you from cheering yourself on is your inner child, who has not yet acknowledged the incredible person you've become and only sees the child. It's time to let the adult in you be your cheerleader—the louder voice, the one who knows what you've been through. As much as it may pain you, tell that inner critic to 'shut up!'

Embracing your role as your own superhero is about more than just waiting for external validation or recognition. It's about recognizing the hero within and acknowledging your own worth. Every person has the potential for greatness, and the journey begins by showing up for yourself. Doing so unlocks hidden potential, fosters resilience, and allows you to lead your life with authenticity.

To reinforce this shift, take the following actions:

- Take a moment to reflect on a time when you failed to show up for yourself.
- How did it impact your well-being, your relationships, or your ability to lead?
- Write down your thoughts.
- Then, identify one way you can show up for yourself this week.

FOR EXAMPLE:
- It could be setting a boundary,
- Taking time for self-care,
- Or celebrating a personal achievement.

Make a commitment to take these actions.

CONFRONTING INTERNAL BARRIERS IS THE NEXT STEP

Fear of being perceived as self-centered or garnering negative reactions from others often holds us back from self-celebration. Yet, every person has the inherent right to revel in their successes, to be their own advocate, and to unabashedly support themselves. You are a significant entity in this vast world, deserving of happiness, fulfillment, and celebration. Recognizing your worth and being your own cheerleader is not an act of arrogance but a fundamental step toward self-nourishment and personal growth.

Becoming your own ally is essential in all areas of life. Befriend yourself, advocate for your own needs, and celebrate your accomplishments. Showing up for yourself is not only a form of self-love but also a foundational pillar for leading a fulfilling and impactful life. Thriving, not just surviving, is the true objective.

As you embrace the power of self-celebration, remember that laughter, cheering, and celebration are acts of empowerment, propelling you forward in the journey of self-discovery and life leadership. The mantra "Show Up for You!" is a resounding affirmation that encapsulates the essence of this journey. It's an invitation to actively participate in your own life, to celebrate personal victories, and to be the hero of your own story. You owe it to yourself, and to those who look up to you, to show up fully, authentically, and unapologetically for yourself.

COMMIT TO BEING YOUR OWN BIGGEST AND GREATEST FAN

Write down three ways you will show up for yourself this month and track your progress. By doing so, you set the stage for a life lived with intention, authenticity, and the courage to be your true self. No matter what, SHOW UP FOR YOU!

CHAPTER ONE REFLECTIONS

Instructions: Reflect on your life experiences and answer the questions honestly and thoughtfully.

DEFINING YOUR HERO

What qualities do you admire in your role models? List specific traits or behaviors.

_____
_____
_____
_____
_____
_____

How do these qualities inspire you to be a better version of yourself?

_____
_____
_____
_____
_____
_____

Describe a time when you exhibited heroic/sheroic qualities, even if it was small.

_____
_____
_____
_____
_____
_____
_____

OVERCOMING CHALLENGES

What are your biggest challenges or fears?

_____
_____
_____
_____
_____
_____

How do these obstacles prevent you from fully embracing your inner hero/shero?

_____
_____
_____
_____
_____
_____

Identify a specific challenge you want to overcome. What steps can you take to conquer it?

_____
_____
_____
_____
_____
_____

BUILDING CONFIDENCE

List your strengths and accomplishments.

_____
_____
_____
_____
_____
_____

How can you build upon these strengths to boost your confidence?

_____
_____
_____
_____
_____
_____

Identify one area where you'd like to improve your confidence. Create a small, achievable goal to work on.

_____
_____
_____
_____
_____
_____

SETTING GOALS

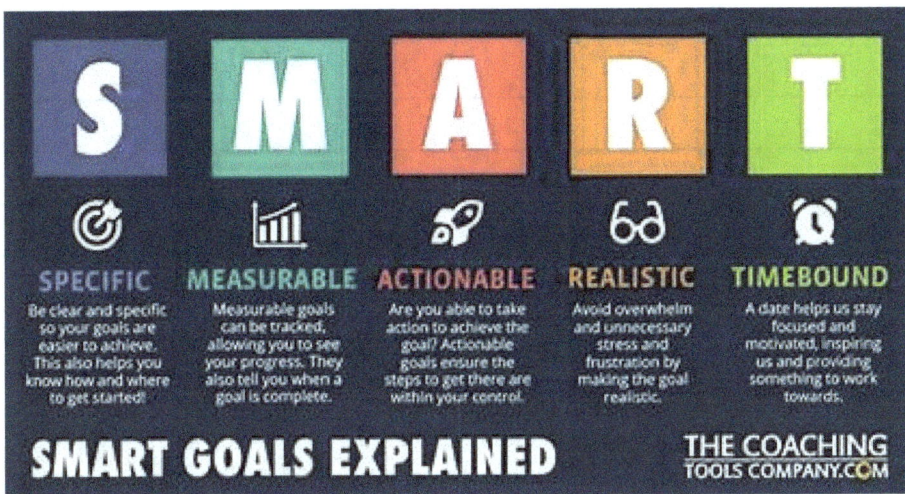

What are your long-term goals?

_____
_____
_____
_____

What steps can you take to achieve these goals?

_____
_____
_____
_____

Break down your goals into smaller, manageable steps.

_____
_____
_____
_____

SELF-CARE

How do you practice self-care?
_____
_____
_____
_____
_____

What activities help you recharge and rejuvenate?

_____
_____
_____
_____
_____

Create a self-care routine that includes physical, emotional, and mental well-being.

_____
_____
_____
_____
_____

AFFIRMATIONS

Write positive affirmations that resonate with you. For example, "I am strong, capable, and worthy." Repeat these affirmations daily to boost your self-esteem.

_____
_____
_____
_____
_____
_____
_____
_____
_____
_____
_____
_____
_____
_____
_____
_____
_____
_____
_____
_____
_____
_____
_____
_____
_____
_____

ACTION PLAN

Choose one specific action step from this worksheet to focus on. Set a deadline for completing this action step. Identify potential obstacles and develop strategies to overcome them.

Remember: Your journey to becoming your own hero/shero is a process. Be patient with yourself and celebrate small victories along the way.

ADDITIONAL TIPS:

Find a supportive community or mentor to encourage your growth. Visualize yourself as the hero/shero you aspire to be. Learn from setbacks and use them as opportunities for growth.

By completing this reflection exercise, you'll gain valuable insights into your strengths, challenges, and goals. Take action on your plan, and you'll be well on your way to embracing your inner hero/shero.

ACTION PLAN

ACTION PLAN

ACTION PLAN

PERSONAL NOTES

PERSONAL NOTES

PERSONAL NOTES

SHOW UP FOR YOU

How do you plan to show up for yourself this month? It's time to set the stage. Get your pad and pen to outline your action steps for this month.

"It's time to break free from the constraints of societal and personal expectations and actively choose self-celebration as a means of empowerment."
-Show Up for You

Key Takeaways

- Recognize the power of the present moment.
- Confront internal barriers.
- Commit to being your biggest fan.

Chapter 2
Created to Be You
Perfect Picture of Humanity

In a world that often values conformity, it's easy to overlook the true strength that lies in your individuality. Every person is a singular masterpiece, thoughtfully crafted with distinct talents, gifts, and characteristics that make them unique. Your existence is not an accident; it is a deliberate part of the intricate fabric of humanity.

Rather than blending in or comparing yourself to others, it's time to embrace and celebrate what sets you apart. The world doesn't need another imitation; it needs the genuine, irreplaceable you. Your journey, your experiences, and your perspective add a richness to the world that no one else can provide.

As you navigate through life, it's essential to recognize that your value isn't determined by how well you measure up to others, but by how fully you embrace and express your true self. You are not just another face in the crowd; you are a vibrant, indispensable part of the human experience. Every detail of who you are has been intentionally designed to contribute to the grand tapestry of life.

From the very beginning, there was a purposeful design—a divine blueprint that set you apart from everyone else. Your talents, gifts, and character traits were not randomly assigned; they were chosen with great care, tailored specifically to contribute to the grand narrative of existence. You are not a mere product of biology, but a deliberate creation, each element of your being carefully considered and placed with intention.

As you begin to fully embrace your individuality, it's important to release the societal pressures of comparison and imitation. In the vast canvas of life, you are not just a brushstroke; you are a masterpiece. Every aspect of your existence is a testament to the intention behind your creation, and within you lies a profound significance that only you can bring to the world.

Consider the diversity of gifts that have been bestowed upon you. Whether it's a natural talent, a unique gift, or a character trait that defines you, each aspect adds to the richness of your individuality. These qualities are not incidental but deliberate components designed to shape your journey and influence the lives of those around you. Recognizing and embracing these traits is more than just an act of self- awareness; it is an acknowledgment of your unique role in the grand design of humanity.

Visualize the world as a vast portrait, with each person contributing a distinct color, creating an overall brilliance that defines the human experience. Your color, your contribution, is irreplaceable. Even in the rare instance of identical twins, their differences in behavior, thoughts, and perspectives highlight the irreplaceable nature of each person. You, too, hold a unique place in this diverse symphony of humanity.

Reflect on your journey and the ways in which your uniqueness has shaped your experiences. How has being true to yourself influenced the paths you've taken, the decisions you've made, and the people you've touched? The beauty of your individuality is that it not only defines you but also enriches the world around you. Embrace the fact that there is no one else like you, and in doing so, you honor the divine intention behind your creation.

This journey of self-exploration invites you to delve deeper into the essence of who you are. By understanding the intention behind your creation, you are encouraged to embrace your talents, cherish your gifts, and celebrate your character traits. In doing so, you not only honor the unique masterpiece that is you but also contribute to the world in a way that only you can.

Your uniqueness is not a flaw; it is your gift to the world. As you move forward, let go of the need to compare yourself to others. Instead, focus on the value you bring simply by being yourself. The world doesn't need another copy; it needs the original that is you. Embrace the understanding that your journey, your experiences, and your perspective are vital components of the collective human story.

As you close this chapter, take a moment to appreciate the person you are. Acknowledge the journey you've been on and the person you've become. Celebrate your strengths, your talents, and even your imperfections, for they all contribute to the masterpiece that is you. You are a perfect picture of humanity, a unique and irreplaceable part of the grand design.

CHAPTER TWO REFLECTIONS

Instructions: How do you value and celebrate your individuality? Look within and complete the reflections below.

SELF-REFLECTION

Take a moment to think about your own uniqueness. What qualities, talents, or experiences make you different from others? Write down at least three aspects that set you apart.

_____

_____

_____

_____

_____

_____

PURPOSE EXPLORATION

Consider what you believe your purpose in life is. What impact do you want to make? Write a brief statement about your purpose or mission.

_____

_____

_____

_____

_____

_____

_____

_____

CANVAS OF AUTHENTICITY

Canvas Metaphor:

Imagine your life as a canvas. What colors, patterns, and textures represent your journey? Draw or describe your canvas—include both the bright moments and the shadows.

CANVAS OF AUTHENTICITY

Scars and Beauty

Our scars—both physical and emotional—tell stories. How have your scars shaped you? Reflect on the beauty that emerges from your imperfections.

_____
_____
_____
_____
_____
_____
_____
_____
_____
_____
_____
_____
_____
_____
_____
_____
_____
_____
_____

REFLECTIONS

DANCING ACROSS LIFE'S STAGE

Your Unique Dance:

Imagine yourself dancing across a grand stage. What moves would you make? What music would play?

Describe your unique dance—whether it's bold, graceful, or quirky.

_____
_____
_____
_____
_____
_____
_____
_____
_____
_____
_____
_____
_____
_____
_____
_____
_____
_____
_____
_____

DANCING ACROSS LIFE'S STAGE

Speaking Your Truth:

How can you use your voice to speak your truth? What messages do you want to share with the world?

Write down a few affirmations or statements that resonate with your soul.

_____

_____

_____

_____

_____

_____

_____

_____

_____

_____

_____

_____

_____

_____

_____

_____

_____

_____

_____

_____

_____

_____

_____

_____

ACTION STEPS

Celebrate Uniqueness:

Identify one way you'll celebrate your uniqueness today. It could be as simple as appreciating a personal quirk or talent.

Write down your action step.

_____
_____
_____
_____
_____
_____
_____
_____
_____
_____
_____
_____
_____
_____
_____
_____
_____
_____
_____

ACTION STEPS

Connect with Purpose:

Consider how you can align your actions with your purpose. What small steps can you take?

List practical actions that move you closer to fulfilling your purpose.

_____
_____
_____
_____
_____
_____
_____
_____
_____
_____
_____
_____
_____
_____
_____
_____
_____
_____
_____
_____
_____
_____
_____

PERSONAL NOTES

PERSONAL NOTES

PERSONAL NOTES

How will you honor the unique masterpiece that you are? You are needed to contribute to the world like only you can.

"The beauty of your individuality is that it not only defines you but also enriches the world around you."
-Show Up for You

Key Takeaways

- Your purpose is powerful.
- Your life is a canvas.
- Affirm your truth and speak it with confidence.

Chapter 3
You Are Needed

When the call to come reaches your ears, it's not just a casual invitation; it's a summons for the authentic you. The people who reach out to you have seen, heard, and experienced something unique that only you can offer. Their request is not an invitation for you to morph into someone else, but rather an expectation for you to show up as your true self. Embracing this truth is vital, as straying from your authentic self can lead to a profound disappointment for those who have specifically called upon you.

Attempting to adopt a persona that you think might align with others' preferences is a misguided approach. It's crucial to recognize that the invitation was extended to you, with all your quirks, perspectives, laughter, and talents. If they wanted someone else, they would have reached out to that person. What they desire is your genuine smile, your unique viewpoint, your valuable input, and the richness of your thoughts.

The notion that your authentic self isn't good enough is a complex and often deeply rooted feeling. This sentiment can stem from various psychological and societal factors that shape how we perceive ourselves. It's essential to understand why some might harbor a sense of inadequacy when it comes to expressing their true selves.

Society often imposes expectations and standards that dictate what is deemed acceptable or desirable. The constant comparison to these external benchmarks can create a sense of inadequacy, leading you to believe that you need to be something other than your true self to be valued. However, the truth is that your authenticity is precisely what makes you valuable.

Fear of rejection and judgment can also play a significant role in inhibiting authenticity. The fear of being misunderstood or facing disapproval often prompts people to suppress or alter aspects of their true selves. But it's important to remember that the invitation extended to you is a recognition of who you genuinely are, not a version of you that conforms to others' expectations.

Past experiences and conditioning can leave lasting imprints on your self-perception. Negative experiences, criticism, or past failures may lead you to believe that your true self is not worthy or acceptable. Over time, this conditioning can contribute to a persistent feeling of not being good enough. Yet, it's precisely these experiences that shape the unique individual you are today.

Internalized perfectionism can set unrealistic standards, creating a perpetual sense of inadequacy. The constant pursuit of flawlessness can make you feel that your authentic self doesn't align with an idealized version of who you should be. But your imperfections are what make you relatable, and they can be the very traits that others appreciate the most.

As you navigate these feelings, it's crucial to shift the narrative from inadequacy to self-compassion and authenticity. Recognize that your authentic self is not only good enough but also inherently valuable and worthy of acceptance. The people who call upon you are seeking the unique qualities that only you possess. By showing up as your true self, you fulfill the very reason they reached out to you in the first place.

Stepping away from your true self not only hinders your ability to respond to a call but also deprives you of the fulfillment and authenticity that you bring to the table. The invitation extended to you is not random; it's a recognition of the unique qualities and perspectives that define you. Understanding this is crucial, as it emphasizes that you possess precisely what those who called upon you are seeking.

Your presence has already inspired and moved those who have witnessed your genuine self. They have been touched in ways that transcend surface impressions. Their desire to learn from you, to share in your gifts and talents, reflects a genuine appreciation for the real, unfiltered you. Presenting anything less than your authentic self in response to this invitation would fall short of the expectations you've already set.

You've made an indelible impression on those who invited you, stirring a desire within them for more and better in their own lives. The call for you to come forth is a testament to the impact you've had, a recognition that your wisdom, inspiration, and authenticity have the power to elevate and transform. They don't want a facsimile; they want you, with all the wisdom and authenticity that accompany your unique journey.

Recognizing the impact of your authenticity is essential. The acknowledgment of your influence is not a mere formality; it's an earnest yearning for you to share your insights directly. You are uniquely qualified to fulfill this request, not as an imitator of someone else, but as the genuine article. No one else can offer what you bring to the table in the same way because your journey, experiences, and perspectives are distinctly yours.

As you take that pivotal step into the spotlight, understand that the desire for your presence extends far beyond a mere want; you are genuinely cherished for the unique individual that you are. This cherished status is not contingent upon a perfected version or a carefully curated persona—it is an embrace of your authenticity, flaws, strengths, and all. Trust in the power of your genuine self to resonate with those who have called upon you.

Your authenticity possesses an inherent power—an ability to transcend surface interactions and delve into the realm of profound connection. In the spotlight, you become not just a figure on display but a catalyst for transformation. Your genuine nature has the potential to serve as a guiding light, teaching others the value of authenticity and inspiring them to embrace their own true selves.

The impact of your authenticity extends beyond the immediate moment; it has the capacity to bring about positive change. By authentically sharing your experiences, insights, and perspectives, you create a ripple effect that reaches into the hearts and minds of those who bear witness. Your authenticity becomes a force for empowerment, encouraging others to navigate their own paths with courage and honesty.

To present an impostor version of yourself is to diminish the potential impact of your unique narrative. It is a disservice to those who recognize and celebrate your authenticity, as well as a disservice to yourself. The richness of your experiences, the authenticity of your voice, and the uniqueness of your perspective collectively contribute to a narrative that cannot be replicated.

Embrace the understanding that you are wonderfully and creatively made. Your journey, with its triumphs and challenges, has uniquely shaped you into the individual you are today. The world eagerly anticipates the genuine, unfiltered version of you—the one that reflects the intricacies of your character and the depth of your being.

So, as you answer the call confidently, know that you are not just stepping into a spotlight; you are stepping into a space where your authenticity is celebrated and revered. Your story, your wisdom, and your authenticity are not only wanted but deeply valued. Step into that spotlight unapologetically, knowing that you are not just wanted—you are needed.

CHAPTER THREE REFLECTIONS

Instructions: By completing the reflections below, you will take a look at leveraging your strengths and addressing your weaknesses.

YOUR UNIQUE QUALITIES

What are your top 5 strengths?

_____
_____
_____
_____
_____

What are you naturally good at?

_____
_____
_____
_____
_____
_____
_____

What are you truly passionate about?

_____
_____
_____
_____
_____
_____

VALUES

What are your core values?

_____
_____
_____
_____
_____
_____
_____
_____
_____
_____
_____
_____
_____
_____
_____
_____
_____
_____
_____
_____
_____
_____

YOUR DESIRED IMPACT

What do you want to achieve in life?

_____
_____
_____
_____
_____
_____

What is your purpose or mission?

_____
_____
_____
_____
_____
_____

How do you want to contribute to the world?

_____
_____
_____
_____
_____
_____

YOUR IDEAL OPPORTUNITIES

Skills Needed:

What skills are required to achieve your goals?

_____
_____
_____
_____
_____
_____
_____

Resources Needed:

What resources do you need to succeed?

_____
_____
_____
_____
_____
_____
_____
_____
_____
_____

YOUR PERSONAL BRAND

What makes you different?

_____
_____
_____
_____
_____
_____

How do your values align with your brand?

_____
_____
_____
_____
_____
_____

Who is your ideal audience or client?

_____
_____
_____
_____
_____
_____
_____

ACTION PLAN

What specific steps can you take to achieve your goals?
_____
_____
_____
_____
_____

When will you take these steps?
_____
_____
_____
_____
_____

What potential obstacles might you face?
_____
_____
_____
_____
_____

IDENTIFYING YOUR VALUE PROPOSITION

Core Competencies:

What are your unique skills and abilities?

_____
_____
_____

Passion Points:

What are you truly passionate about?

_____
_____
_____

Problem-Solving Abilities:

What problems can you solve?

_____
_____
_____

Unique Perspective:

How is your viewpoint different from others?

_____
_____
_____
_____

UNDERSTANDING YOUR TARGET AUDIENCE

Ideal Client/Customer

Who is your ideal recipient?

_____
_____
_____
_____
_____

Needs and Pain Points:

What challenges or problems do they face?

_____
_____
_____
_____
_____

Desires and Goals:

What do they want to achieve?

_____
_____
_____
_____
_____

MATCHING YOUR OFFERINGS

Solution Alignment:

How do your skills and passions address their needs?

_____
_____
_____
_____
_____

Value Proposition:

How does your offering create value for them?

_____
_____
_____
_____
_____

Unique Selling Point:

What sets your offering apart from competitors?

_____
_____
_____
_____
_____

CREATING A COMPELLING OFFER

Clear and Concise Messaging:

How can you clearly communicate your value?

_____
_____
_____
_____
_____

Benefits-Focused:

How does your offering benefit the customer?

_____
_____
_____
_____
_____
_____

Call to Action:

What specific action do you want the customer to take?

_____
_____
_____
_____
_____
_____

DELIVERING EXECPTIONAL VALUE

Customer Focus:

How can you exceed customer expectations?

_____
_____
_____
_____
_____

Feedback Integration:

How will you use customer feedback to improve?

_____
_____
_____
_____
_____
_____

Building Relationships:

How can you foster long-term customer relationships?

_____
_____
_____
_____
_____
_____

DISCOVERING YOUR UNIQUE ABILITIES

Strengths:

What are your top 5 strengths?
___
___
___

Passions:

What are you truly passionate about?
___
___
___

Talents:

What are you naturally good at?
___
___
___

Unique Qualities:

What makes you different from others?
___
___
___
___

IDENTIFYING YOUR TARGET AUDIENCE

Ideal Client/Customer:

Who would benefit from your gifts?

_____
_____
_____
_____
_____

Needs and Desires

What problems or needs can you solve for them?

_____
_____
_____
_____
_____
_____

Platform Preferences:

Where does your target audience spend their time online?

_____
_____
_____
_____
_____
_____

CREATING YOUR PLATFORM

Brand Identity:

How do you want to present yourself?

_____
_____
_____
_____
_____

Content Creation:

What type of content will you create (blog posts, videos, etc.)?

_____
_____
_____
_____
_____

Platform Selection:

Which platforms will you use to share your content?

_____
_____
_____
_____
_____

BUILDING YOUR AUDIENCE

Engagement Strategies:

How will you interact with your audience?

_____
_____
_____
_____
_____

Community Building:

How will you create a sense of community?

_____
_____
_____
_____
_____
_____

Collaboration:

How can you collaborate with others in your field?

_____
_____
_____
_____
_____
_____

MEASURING YOUR IMPACT

Goals:

What do you want to achieve with your platform?

_____
_____
_____
_____
_____

Metrics:

How will you measure your success?

_____
_____
_____
_____
_____
_____

Adjustments:

How will you adapt your strategy based on results?

_____
_____
_____
_____
_____
_____

Remember: Sharing your gifts with the world is a journey, not a destination. Be patient, persistent, and authentic. You have unique talents and abilities that the world needs. Believe in yourself and take steps to share your gifts with the world. Your value is unique and in demand. By clearly identifying your offerings and understanding your audience, you can effectively deliver what they need.

PERSONAL NOTES

PERSONAL NOTES

PERSONAL NOTES

How will you use your authentic voice to contribute to a narrative that cannot be replicated?

"Your genuine nature has the potential to serve as a guiding light, teaching others the value of authenticity and inspiring them to embrace their own true selves."
-Show Up for You

Key Takeaways

- Your unique qualities and values matter.
- Your differences create your personal brand.
- The world needs you to share your gifts.

Chapter 4

The Strength of Imperfection
Embracing Your True Self

In a society that often idolizes perfection, the idea of embracing our imperfections can feel counterintuitive. Yet, it is in these very imperfections that our true beauty and strength lie. To be unapologetically yourself means to embrace every facet of who you are—flaws, quirks, strengths, and all. It's about showing up in the world without pretense, with the understanding that your worth isn't diminished by your imperfections but rather enhanced by them.

When you allow yourself to be truly seen, without the masks that society often pressures us to wear, you create space for genuine connection and understanding. Being real isn't about having it all together; it's about acknowledging your weaknesses and vulnerabilities. Instead of hiding them, you share them as part of your journey. This openness is not a sign of weakness, but of incredible strength, as it takes courage to show up as you are, without the need to impress or conform.

Imperfections are often viewed as shortcomings, but they are, in fact, valuable lessons that shape your character and influence your path. Every imperfection you possess tells a story—a story of growth, resilience, and the human experience. These imperfections provide insights not only for you but also for those around you. When you share your imperfections, you offer others a guide for navigating their own challenges.

To redefine imperfections, it's essential to challenge the conventional notion that they are obstacles to be overcome. Instead, view them as integral components of your story—chapters that contribute to the richness of your life. By accepting and embracing your imperfections, you create a narrative that is relatable, empowering, and full of depth. One that gives you a powerful authentic self. Not to mention a powerful testimony!

Sharing the journey of navigating and overcoming imperfections fosters a deeper connection with others. It's not just about showcasing polished outcomes but about revealing the struggles, setbacks, and lessons learned along the way. This openness creates an environment where others feel safe to share their own stories, leading to a more meaningful connection.

Consider the impact of your personal journey on those who witness it. The wisdom gained through embracing and overcoming your imperfections becomes a beacon of hope for others on similar paths. By sharing your experiences, you offer a sense of solidarity and encouragement to those grappling with their own challenges. Your journey becomes not just your story but a source of inspiration for those around you.

When we acknowledge that what one person perceives as an imperfection may deeply resonate with someone else facing similar struggles, we reinforce the collective nature of human experience. Your willingness to be open about your imperfections connects you to others on a profound level, reminding them that they are not alone in their journeys.

THERE IS IMMENSE POWER IN VULNERABILITY

Success is often portrayed as a series of flawless achievements, but true success lies in the courage to embrace and share your imperfections. This openness can be a powerful force for personal growth and community building. By being unapologetically yourself, you encourage others to do the same.

This perspective invites a reevaluation of how we perceive success and personal growth. It shifts the focus from external validation to internal fulfillment. Success is not solely determined by outward achievements, but by the internal journey of self- discovery, resilience, and growth. It's about thriving, not in spite of your imperfections, but because of them.

Recognizing that your vulnerabilities can be a source of strength is central to this shift. Your willingness to share your imperfections openly demonstrates a confidence that is both inspiring and contagious. It allows for genuine connections, fostering a sense of shared humanity and mutual understanding.

As you embrace your true self, you create a foundation for continuous self- improvement and resilience. This journey is not a static state but a dynamic process of growth and evolution. By accepting and embracing your imperfections, you open the door to a deeper understanding of yourself and others.

Beyond individual empowerment, the act of sharing your journey has a broader impact on community building. By openly discussing your imperfections, you contribute to the creation of communities that are genuine, supportive, and understanding. Imperfections are reframed as shared experiences that unite individuals, fostering a collective strength that transcends individual struggles.

RELATABILITY IS A TRANSFORMATIVE FORCE

When you share the journey of embracing your imperfections, you become more relatable and approachable. This relatability creates bridges of understanding between people, breaking down barriers and fostering a culture of empathy and encouragement.

By embracing and sharing your imperfections, you contribute to a culture where diverse experiences are celebrated. This culture of empathy and encouragement flourishes when individuals recognize that imperfections are part of the shared human experience. Encouragement becomes a communal practice, supporting each other on the journey of growth and self-acceptance.

In essence, your imperfections are not just parts of you to be hidden away; they are integral to the beauty of your whole being. By embracing them, you allow others to see the real you—a person who is relatable, resilient, and inspiring. Your imperfections are what make you human, and in sharing them, you build a legacy of courage and honesty.

As you continue on this journey, remember that you are not alone. Every person you meet has their own set of imperfections, their own story of struggle and triumph. By showing up as unapologetically you, you give others permission to do the same. Together, we create a world where diversity of experience is celebrated, and imperfections are embraced as the valuable teachings they are.

CHAPTER FOUR REFLECTIONS

Instructions: These reflections are a journey of self-discovery. It's about understanding who you are, what you value, and what makes you unique. Let's explore your true self!

SELF-REFLECTION

My Core Values: What principles guide your life?
_____
_____

My Strengths: What are you naturally good at?
_____
_____

My Weaknesses: What areas do you want to improve?
_____
_____

My Passions: What truly excites and motivates you?
_____
_____

My Goals: What do you want to achieve in life?
_____
_____

DISCOVERING YOUR IDENTITY

My Personality:

Describe your personality using 5 words. What makes you stand out from the crowd?

_____
_____
_____
_____

My Values in Action:

How do your core values show up in your daily life?

_____
_____
_____
_____
_____
_____

Overcoming Challenges:

How do you handle obstacles in your path?

_____
_____
_____
_____
_____
_____

BUILDING SELF-CONFIDENCE

Positive Affirmations:

Write 5 positive statements about yourself.
_____
_____
_____

Celebrating Achievements:

List 3 accomplishments you're proud of.
_____
_____
_____

Learning from Mistakes:

How have past failures helped you grow?
_____
_____
_____

Self-Care:

What do you do to relax and recharge?
_____
_____
_____
_____

EMBRACING YOUR TRUE SELF

Authenticity:

In what areas of your life do you feel most authentic?

_____
_____
_____
_____

Personal Growth:

How can you continue to develop your true self?

_____
_____
_____
_____
_____

Inspiring Others:

How can you share your authentic self with others?

_____
_____
_____
_____
_____

REFLECTIONS

What did you learn about yourself through this worksheet?

_____
_____
_____
_____
_____
_____
_____
_____

How can you incorporate your true self into your daily life?

_____
_____
_____
_____
_____
_____
_____
_____

Remember: Your true self is a beautiful and complex tapestry. Embrace it wholeheartedly!

REFLECTIONS

PERSONAL NOTES

PERSONAL NOTES

PERSONAL NOTES

What imperfections are you willing to be open about? How might your transparency impact others on their journey?

"Your willingness to be open about your imperfections connects you to others on a profound level, reminding them that they are not alone in their journeys."
-Show Up for You

Key Takeaways

- There is power in your vulnerability.
- Your relatability has a transformative force.
- When you show up as yourself you give others permission to do the same.

Chapter 5

Your Voice Must Be Heard

In a world where silence can lead to being overlooked, it's crucial to recognize the power of your voice—especially as a leader. If you withhold your thoughts and refrain from speaking up, your impact may diminish, and the unique contribution you have to offer could be lost. As a leader, your voice is an invaluable asset, not only within the teams you lead but also in shaping the broader culture of your organization, community, or family. By allowing your voice to resonate, you don't just participate in conversations; you shape them, enrich them, and help drive meaningful change.

When you speak up as a leader, you're not just contributing to the dialogue—you're asserting your presence in the world. Every opinion, thought, and perspective you share adds a layer of richness to the collective understanding. If you choose to remain silent, you risk fading into the background, and the distinctive value you bring may go unnoticed. Your voice holds the potential to influence, inspire, and effect positive change within your organization and beyond. Speaking out is not just an option; it is a responsibility—one that ensures your unique insights and leadership shape the narrative and direction of the teams and communities you serve.

In the vast sea of voices, yours stands out as a critical and valuable contributor. Effective communication is the cornerstone of any thriving organization or team. As a leader, your voice can be the catalyst for innovation, the solution to problems, or the key to fostering deeper connections among your peers. Your communication acts as a bridge that connects you with others, creating a space for collaboration and mutual understanding.

Moreover, speaking up is not just about being heard by others; it's also a powerful means of building your own confidence as a leader. Each time you express your thoughts, you affirm your leadership and your ability to guide others. Over time, this practice strengthens your self-assurance—a trait that is foundational for effective leadership. Imagine the profound impact your voice might have on another person's life. When you share your thoughts openly, you may unknowingly inspire and influence others. Your unique perspective might resonate with someone else, encouraging them to see things in a new light or emboldening them to voice their own opinions. Your words can serve as a catalyst for positive change, not just in your organization but in the lives of those you lead.

The power of your voice as a leader goes beyond tangible outcomes. The ability to inspire and motivate others through your words is a priceless gift. Your voice can be the source of encouragement that propels your team forward, fostering a mindset of resilience and determination. This influence extends far beyond material successes; it is a legacy of wisdom and inspiration that you leave behind. By speaking out, you contribute to the creation of a culture where diverse opinions are not just welcomed but celebrated. This inclusive environment fosters creativity, mutual respect, and a sense of belonging, essential elements of a thriving organizational culture. Your willingness to share empowers others to do the same, creating a positive cycle of open communication within your leadership sphere.

CONSIDER YOUR VOICE AS A TOOL TO LEAVE A LASTING LEGACY

The thoughts and opinions you express today can echo through time, influencing the future of your organization and the lives of those you mentor and lead. Your willingness to share your true self sets a powerful example for others to follow. In this way, your voice becomes a part of a larger narrative, shaping the collective consciousness and the culture of your organization for the better.

In a world where information flows rapidly and attention spans are fleeting, being seen and heard is the key to making a lasting impact as a leader. Regardless of your position, the visibility of your voice contributes to your recognition and influence. This visibility extends beyond personal gain; it positions you to shape narratives, influence decisions, and contribute meaningfully to the lives of those around you. Navigating a noisy world can be challenging, but this only heightens the importance of not muting your own voice. Every leader has a unique perspective to offer, and allowing your voice to be heard becomes a way to cut through the noise and make a distinct mark.

The ripple effect of your voice extends far beyond personal interactions. On a local scale, your voice can influence and impact communities, driving change and improvement. This impact is not limited by geographic boundaries; your voice has the potential to transcend communities, influencing projects, proposals, and initiatives.

Recognizing your right to use your voice as a tool for impact is empowering. Every leader possesses the agency to contribute to discussions, decisions, and societal narratives. Your voice is not just a personal expression; it is a vehicle for change and a catalyst for progress. Furthermore, acknowledging that not everyone gets the chance or opportunity to have their voice heard underscores your responsibility to speak not just for yourself but on behalf of those who may be marginalized or silenced. This advocacy extends the impact of your voice, turning it into a force for equity, justice, and representation within your organization and beyond.

Geddy Lee's words, "The only way to make your voice heard is to use it," and "Do not be afraid to speak up for what you believe in, even if your voice shakes, let it serves as a powerful motivational anchor. These quotes reinforce the idea that overcoming fear and hesitation is essential in making a meaningful contribution through your voice as a leader.

Voices have been compared to fingerprints, each unique and irreplaceable. No two voices are identical, and this diversity should be celebrated. Recognize and embrace the distinctive qualities of your voice, understanding that it adds a valuable dimension to the collective conversation and the culture of your organization.

As we come to the close of this journey, I leave you with one powerful, resonating challenge: YOUR VOICE MUST BE HEARD! Open your mouth and speak now. Let us hear you!" This is not just a call for self-expression; it is a call for you to fully step into your power, to embrace the stage of your life and leadership with confidence and conviction.

This is your moment—your opportunity to show up for yourself and your team in the most profound way. Your voice, your thoughts, your presence—they all matter. Whether you are leading a family, a team, a community, or an organization, your voice is the instrument through which you can shape the world around you. Do not let fear or doubt hold you back. Open your mouth, speak your truth, and let the world witness the strength that comes from being unapologetically you.

As you walk away from these pages, remember that the journey of showing up for yourself doesn't end here. It begins anew every day with every choice you make to honor your voice, your leadership, and your unique place in the world. The world needs you to show up, not just for others but for yourself. Your voice is not just wanted; it is needed. So, go forth with courage, and remember: Show Up for You.

CHAPTER FIVE REFLECTIONS

Instructions: Everyone has a unique perspective to share. These reflections will help you explore your voice, understand its importance, and find ways to make it heard.

UNDERSTANDING YOUR VOICE

Core Values: What principles guide your communication? What are your communication strengths?

_____
_____
_____
_____
_____

Areas for Improvement: What areas would you like to develop?

_____
_____
_____
_____
_____

Communication Style: How would you describe your communication style?

_____
_____
_____
_____
_____

FINDING YOUR AUDIENCE

Target Audience:

Who are you trying to reach?

_____
_____
_____
_____
_____

Needs and Interests:

What are their needs and interests?

_____
_____
_____
_____
_____

Communication Channels:

What platforms are best to reach your audience?

_____
_____
_____
_____
_____

CRAFTING YOUR MESSAGE

Key Message:

What is the core message you want to convey?

_____
_____
_____
_____
_____
_____
_____
_____
_____

Supporting Points:

What evidence or examples support your message?

_____
_____
_____
_____
_____
_____
_____
_____
_____

DELIVERING YOUR MESSAGE

Overcoming Fear:

What challenges do you face when speaking up?

_____
_____
_____
_____
_____
_____
_____
_____

Building Confidence:

How can you increase your confidence?

_____
_____
_____
_____
_____
_____
_____
_____

DELIVERING YOUR MESSAGE

Practice and Feedback:

How can you improve your delivery?

___

Remember: Your voice is a powerful tool. Use it wisely and effectively to make a difference.

MEASURING IMPACT

Goals:

What do you hope to achieve with your message?

_____
_____
_____
_____
_____
_____
_____
_____

Metrics:

How will you measure the success of your message?

_____
_____
_____
_____
_____
_____
_____
_____
_____

LEARNING AND GROWTH

Learning and Growth:

How can you improve for future communications?

_____
_____
_____
_____
_____
_____
_____
_____
_____
_____
_____
_____
_____
_____
_____
_____
_____
_____
_____
_____
_____
_____
_____

Remember: Your voice is a powerful tool. Use it wisely and effectively to make a difference.

DISCOVERING YOUR VOICE

What I Value:

What are the core beliefs and principles that guide your life?
_____
_____
_____

My Passions:

What are you truly passionate about?
_____
_____
_____

My Strengths:

What are your talents and abilities?
_____
_____
_____

My Experiences:

What life experiences have shaped your worldview?
_____
_____
_____
_____

FINDING YOUR VOICE

Overcoming Fear:

What holds you back from expressing your voice?

_____
_____
_____
_____
_____
_____
_____
_____
_____
_____

Building Confidence:

How can you build confidence in your ability to communicate?

_____
_____
_____
_____
_____
_____
_____
_____

FINDING YOUR AUDIENCE

Who do you want to reach with your message?

MAKING YOUR VOICE HEARD

Communication Channels:

What platforms or methods can you use to share your message?

_____
_____
_____
_____

Creating Impact:

How can you make your message meaningful and impactful?

_____
_____
_____
_____
_____
_____

Taking Action:

What specific steps can you take to share your voice?

_____
_____
_____
_____
_____
_____

LISTENING AND LEARNING

Active Listening:

How can you improve your listening skills?

_____
_____
_____
_____
_____

Seeking Feedback:

How can you get constructive feedback on your message?

_____
_____
_____
_____
_____

Continuous Learning:

What steps can you take to continue developing your voice?

_____
_____
_____
_____
_____

REFLECTIONS

What did you learn about yourself and your voice through this worksheet? How will you use this newfound knowledge to make a difference?

Remember: Your voice matters. Use it to inspire, inform, and create positive change.

_____
_____
_____
_____
_____
_____
_____
_____
_____
_____
_____
_____
_____
_____
_____
_____
_____
_____
_____
_____
_____
_____
_____

PERSONAL NOTES

PERSONAL NOTES

PERSONAL NOTES

How will you use your voice and fully step into your power to embrace the stage of your life with confidence?

"This is your moment—your opportunity to show up for yourself and your team in the most profound way. Your voice, your thoughts, your presence—they all matter."
-Show Up for You

Key Takeaways

- Your voice is unique and provides a unique perspective.
- Your voice is a source of encouragement.
- Your voice is not wanted, it is needed.

Conclusion

YOUR JOURNEY BEGINS NOW

As you reach the end of this book, remember that the insights and reflections you've encountered here are not merely words on a page; they are calls to action. The journey of showing up for yourself is ongoing, one that requires intention, commitment, and courage. The pages you've read are the beginning, not the end, of a transformative process that has the potential to profoundly impact not only your life but the lives of those you lead.

CALL TO ACTION: SHOW UP FULLY

Now is the time to take what you've learned and put it into action. As a leader, whether in your home, your workplace, your family, your community, your voice, your presence, and your authenticity are needed more than ever. Reflect on the lessons and strategies discussed in this book and identify specific actions you can take to show up more fully in your leadership roles.

START BY MAKING A COMMITMENT TO YOURSELF.

Choose one area of your life where you've been holding back, where you've allowed fear or doubt to silence your voice. Decide today that you will step into that space with confidence and intention. Maybe it's speaking up more in meetings, advocating for your team with greater conviction, or simply giving yourself the grace to be imperfect yet powerful.

WRITE DOWN YOUR COMMITMENTS

Hold yourself accountable. Share them with a trusted colleague, friend, or mentor who can support you in your journey. Remember, the goal is not to achieve perfection but to embrace the ongoing process of growth, learning, and self- discovery. By showing up fully, you set an example for others, creating a ripple effect that encourages those around you to do the same.

FINAL INSPIRATIONAL MESSAGE: YOU ARE UNIQUELY VALUABLE

As you move forward, never forget the unique value you bring to the world. There is no one else with your exact combination of experiences, insights, and gifts. Your perspective is irreplaceable, and your contributions are essential to the fabric of the communities and organizations you are part of.

The world needs leaders who are not afraid to be themselves—leaders who recognize the strength in vulnerability, the power of their voice, and the impact of their authenticity. You are that leader. You have the ability to shape the future, to inspire change, and to leave a lasting legacy simply by being true to who you are.

So, step into your role with confidence. Embrace your journey with courage. Show up for yourself in every area of your life, knowing that when you do, you empower others to do the same. The path ahead may not always be easy, but it will be worth the journey. Your authentic presence is your greatest gift to the world, and it is through this presence that you will make the most profound difference.

This book is a culmination of my years of experiences, mistakes, and proven leadership practices that have led me to confidently "SHOW UP FOR ME." Each chapter is a reflection of my personal journey. I share this book from my heart to yours, because I want you to understand the importance to 'SHOW UP FOR YOU.' As you close this book, carry this truth with you: You are needed. Your voice matters. Your leadership can change the world. Now, go forth and show up for you— because when you do, you show up for all of us. It's time!

Your leadership can save the world!

MEET THE AUTHOR

Dr. Judy Mandrell is the proud and happy wife of Superintendent Dr. Gerald Mandrell for over 42 years. Dr. Judy Mandrell's mantra is: "If, I can help somebody as I travel this life, then my living will not be in vain." She has a faith that turns dreams into reality for herself and others. She is a path maker. Her genuineness, love, compassion, and joy are felt by everyone she touches throughout the community, the city, the state, and internationally. Dr. Judy Mandrell authentically, untiringly, and wholeheartedly serves both her church and community. Her genuineness, love, passion, and joy are felt throughout her community, city and by everyone she touches. She works closely alongside her husband of over 41 years, Senior Pastor, Dr. Gerald Mandrell at Life Changers COGIC.

She is a God ordained, called and anointed evangelist in the Lord's church. She is an international speaker, one of her most humble speaking opportunities was being the keynote speaker at THE CHURCH OF THE HOLY RUDE in Sterling, Scotland, where King James was baptized, King Charles and many other Kings were crowned.

She is incomparably one of the most life-changing loving influential women in the world. She travels extensively throughout the United Stated both as an evangelist and conference speaker to many churches, businesses and organizations. Her love, support, and powerful presence in the community and in the church is phenomenal. She is a leaders' leader; and a "PEOPLE'S ARCHITECT."

Dr. Mandrell organized over 500 Tallahassee women across race, economics, religion, political party, social status and brought them together to get to know each other, and they are still meeting quarterly.

Dr. Mandrell, at the leading of the Holy Spirit, has brought 60 pastors and their congregations together from various denomination since December 2022, to meet every Monday after the 1st Sunday to pray for Tallahassee and have gone to very spot where a person has been killed by gun violence in Tallahassee with Pastors, intercessors and prayer warriors to pray for the victim family and the shooter family. Tallahassee, FL has caught on fire with this prayer.

She has received so many rewards, recognitions, and awards for her untiring service to the church and the community.

- RECEIVED THE KEY TO THE CITY of Tallahassee, FL
- PRESIDENT LIFETIME ACHIEVEMENT AWARD
- W.E.B. DUBOIS HUMANITARIAN AWARD
- 2023 Greater Tallahassee Chambers of Commerce Leader of the Year
- John Maxwell Stellar Leadership Award
- 2020 John Maxwell Certified Coach, Trainer, and Speaker
- Tallahassee Democrat 25 Women You Need to Know Award

Dr. Mandrell has spent her life serving by empowering, inspiring, and making pathways for others to follow. She is a true trailblazer.

GET IN TOUCH

Website: showupforyou.com
Email: Judyshowupforyou@gmail.com
Facebook: @JudyShowUpForYou
Instagram: @JudyShowUpForYou
YouTube: @JudyShowUpForYou

When you "SHOW UP FOR YOU," be prepared to enter the arena with substance. Part of authenticity is being true to your strengths and aware of what needs to be further developed or enhance to make you the best you can be.

-Ms. Anita Favors

www.ingramcontent.com/pod-product-compliance
Lightning Source LLC
Chambersburg PA
CBHW070336230426
43663CB00011B/2334